Affordable PARIS HOTELS

A Travel Smart Mini-Guide

CAROLINE O'CONNELL

Travel Smart Press

Published 2025
Printed in the United States of America

Paperback ISBN: 979-8-9926164-0-8
Ebook ISBN: 979-8-9926164-1-5

Travel Smart Press, Los Angeles, CA
www.TravelSmartPress.com

Cover design by Marianne Nowicki
Interior design and typeset by Andrea Reider
Photos by Caroline O'Connell
Map data from ©OpenStreetMap (OSM):
www.OpenStreetMap.org/copyright

CONTENTS

Seine River / Île de la Cité

INTRODUCTION

"Paris is always a good idea," the oft-quoted saying goes. There are many reasons why this magical city is the top travel destination in the world.

It's beautiful. In addition to parks adjacent numerous churches and monuments in the center of the city, you'll find the much larger Tuileries Gardens on the Right Bank, facing the Louvre Museum, and the Luxembourg Gardens on the Left Bank.

There are world-class sites. From the breathtaking Impressionist paintings at Musée d'Orsay, to the opulent Opéra Garnier concert hall, to the celebration of haute couture at Galeries Dior, there are dozens of amazing venues that are one-of-a-kind.

Monuments showcasing Paris's history frame the skyline. The iconic Eiffel Tower has become a symbol for travel itself. The nearby Arc de Triomphe stands watch over the grand Avenue des Champs-Élysées. Notre-Dame, on the larger island, represents the heartbeat of Paris.

All this wonderful culture comes with a price—crowds competing for the same accommodations. My top two recommendations are to stay in the center of the city adjacent the Seine River, where these sites are a short walk away, and to book your trip "off season" when the prices are lower and the crowds have thinned.

For research on this book and my previous Paris guides, I combed the city seeking out lovely areas that put you in the center of the action. Some neighborhoods are upscale, and some are more residential, but they're all "pinch myself I'm in Paris" charming.

Criteria

First and foremost, all the hotels in this guide are near top attractions and quintessentially Parisian cafés and boutiques. From the moment you step outside the lobby door, you'll feel like you're stepping into a movie (or a TV show— *Emily in Paris* comes to mind).

Second, a trip to Paris is expensive enough without spending a fortune on your room. But a budget hotel could diminish the joy of your trip. The three-star hotels in this guide are the sweet spot. They're reasonably priced (by Paris's standards) and offer lovely accommodations. A few four-star hotels with moderate rates are also included.

What the Three-Star Rating Means

French hotels are awarded stars based on more than two hundred criteria. For each rating, some items are mandatory and others are optional. For example, room size is mandatory— meaning at each star level the rooms become a bit larger. Rooms in three-star hotels must have an *en suite* bathroom, and three-star hotels with four or more floors must have an elevator. There could still be steps to reach the elevator.

To stay competitive, three-star hotels have invested in attractive décor and furnishings, luxurious linens, and inviting lobbies and breakfast rooms. Instead of paying 450 euros per night for a deluxe four-star experience, you can find rooms at three-star hotels for under 300 euros per night (and sometimes under 250 euros, depending on the month).

What's Covered in This Guide

Each chapter starts with a description of the district and why it's included. All the areas are within walking distance of the Seine River in the center of Paris. The number of listings in each chapter varies, depending on how many hotels in that area fit the criteria. Saint-Germain-des-Prés (in the sixth arrondissement) is chock-full of charming hotels, so it takes up three chapters.

The listings include all the details you'll need: name of hotel, address, phone number, website, and brief description (info in quotation marks is from the hotel). There are also maps (by arrondissement) showing where the hotels are located, and photos are sprinkled throughout.

The Ten Areas

- Palais Royal/Louvre
- St. Honoré/Tuileries
- Opéra Garnier
- Marais/Île Saint-Louis
- Latin Quarter
- Left Bank Near Seine River
- Left Bank Near Blvd. St. Germain
- Place Saint-Sulpice/Luxembourg Gardens
- Musée d'Orsay
- Eiffel Tower

During Your Stay

One of the important benefits of staying in a hotel, rather than booking an apartment, is that they have staff on the premises twenty-four hours a day. The front desk personnel are trained to speak English and assist you with navigating your stay in Paris. Take advantage of their expertise and services. They will:

- Stock complimentary fold-out street maps
- Recommend places for dinner and/or make a reservation
- Provide fliers about current activities, including classical music concerts in nearby churches
- Call a taxi for you
- Store your luggage

The four-star hotels I've included offer more amenities, like a bar/lounge, beautiful public spaces, a restaurant on the premises, and possibly a spa or gym.

How To Use This Guide

All the information is current at the time of publication. To check on more recent developments, every hotel's website is listed. To find a specific hotel, there is an Index at the back of this guide by name of hotel in alphabetical order.

Lastly, to receive a free booklet on Paris Packing Tips that explains how to look glamorous in the City of Light, while traveling light, go to this link: www.CarolineOC.com. The booklet includes airline regulations, tips, sample wardrobe ideas, and a checklist.

Bon voyage,

Caroline O' Connell

BOOKING A HOTEL ROOM

When to Take Your Trip

If you have a choice, I recommend traveling in off season, when it's less expensive and less crowded. My preference—the months of April, May, September, October, and November. Yes, some of those months are cooler, and it could rain, but the streets are magical when you're among Parisians. The holidays are a festive time, but hotel prices go up due to high demand, and it will be cold (an excuse to bundle up in your fancy winter attire).

When to Book

Reserve as far ahead as you can, ideally six months before the trip. These are smaller boutique hotels that fill up early, and room rates go up closer to the actual date. Always reserve a room that you can cancel (unless it's last minute; then you can take advantage of the cheaper nonrefundable rate).

Shop Around

If you want to research on your own, start on an aggregator site, like Booking.com, where you see a number of options. At a glance, you'll have an idea of general availability for your dates and the price range at that time. Then you can check out the hotel website to see if they are offering better rates (or free breakfast). Most hotels will give the best price on their websites, but not always. I have a "Genius" level on Booking, so they occasionally give me better deals (10% off, free breakfast, or upgrade to a better room).

Look at the photos. You will get a good idea of the décor, style, size of the room, quality of the bathroom, bed linens, window size, all kinds of things. My friend Andrea, an artist, requested a specific room that she saw on the hotel's website, since each room had a unique design. They complied, and she was very happy with her stay.

Criteria To Consider

- Do they have air conditioning?
- Do they have a minibar and coffeemaker in the room?
- Is there a safe?
- What is the size of the room?
- Does the elevator go to all the rooms?

A Note About Room Size

Many guest reviewers complain about the size of their hotel rooms. Real estate in Paris is at a premium and these are centuries-old buildings. Hotel rooms will be smaller than travelers are accustomed to. Most booking sites give the exact dimensions (square feet) of each room type, so take that into consideration if it's important to you.

A Note About Stairs

Sometimes rooms on the highest floors are reached by a flight of stairs. In smaller hotels, you may need to take stairs to reach the elevator. And many hotels have one or more steps to enter the hotel. Again, these are old buildings.

A tip: If you're traveling solo, Single Rooms are less expensive. It's usually a twin bed in a teeny, tiny space on the top floor, but you can use the euros you save for a shopping splurge.

Making Your Reservation

All hotels require a credit card to confirm the reservation. Many times, they will charge the first night's stay as a deposit (that is refundable if you cancel within their required time frame). Check your cancellation policy thoroughly and make a note on your calendar. If you do get a non-refundable room, you will save money (up to 25%), but I only recommend this when it's close to your departure date.

Here are general room categories (not counting suites and connecting family rooms). As you can see, they are related to room size:

> *Classique* – the entry level room, smaller, but with the same décor and bed linens as the other room types

> *Superieure* – a bigger room, usually a sitting area or desk, a bit more luxurious

> *Deluxe* – the nicest rooms, might have a balcony or a separate sitting area

Breakfast at the Hotel

One option is to grab coffee and a croissant at a nearby café each morning, which I used to recommend. Now I prefer the convenience of having breakfast in the hotel in charming surroundings, especially in inclement weather. Most hotels go out of their way to provide a good selection; more than you would get for the same price at a café (i.e. coffee or tea, pastries, juice, yogurt, cereal, possibly eggs and cheese—for one flat rate).

When you start your day in the breakfast room, the hotel feels more like a home and you get to know the staff. Also, you have the option to grab a pastry or piece of fruit to eat later.

I'm a firm believer in having a few snacks in the room. One hotel I researched has a policy of not allowing any food in the room, so I excluded them from this guide.

If the breakfast price seems high, you can wait until you arrive to decide if you want to add that to your reservation.

A Reminder

Finally, always reconfirm with the hotel a week before to make sure there aren't any hiccups in your reservation; mention your dates, room type, etc. The easiest way is to email the hotel. You'll find they're very responsive.

CHAPTER ONE

PALAIS ROYAL/LOUVRE

Once the home of kings, this district boasts the Louvre Museum, the lovely (hidden) Palais Royal Garden, and the starting point of Rue St. Honoré, a famous street lined with designer stores. Keep in mind that the area can be bustling with crowds, since so many people are there to visit the Louvre; it's not as quiet as other neighborhoods in the guide.

This is one of the most expensive districts in Paris, and hotel prices reflect that. I was able to find a number of charming hotels at affordable rates.

> Hôtel de la Place du Louvre
> Hôtel Elixir
> Hôtel Louvre Piemont
> Hôtel Louvre Sainte-Anne
> Hôtel Montpensier
> Hôtel Thérèse
> Timhotel Palais Royal

Statue of Jeanne d'Arc

HÔTEL DE LA PLACE DU LOUVRE ★ ★ ★ ★

21 Rue des Prêtres St. Germain l'Auxerrois
1st arrondissement
Phone: 01 42 33 78 68
www.paris-hotel-place-du-louvre.com

This hotel is housed in a seventeenth-century building near Saint-Germain l'Auxerrois Church, an even older building, whose construction began in the twelfth-century. We're talking history.

In addition to lovely rooms and service, the hotel has an excellent guide to nearby locales on their website (under Neighborhood). For a four-star hotel, the prices are reasonable.

HÔTEL ELIXIR ★ ★ ★

7 Rue Jean Lantier
1st arrondissement
Phone: 01 42 33 45 38
https://hotelelixir.com/en/

A newly renovated boutique hotel, the rooms are small and basic, no frills, with modern décor (they call it "contemporary"). The updated bathrooms are small and have colorful mosaic tiles. Rooms have a minibar and Nespresso machine.

Prices are good for Paris—a basic double room for around 150 euros in off season. Although it's technically in the first arrondissement, it's on the far east end, closer to the fourth arrondissement, near the bridge to Notre-Dame.

HÔTEL LOUVRE PIEMONT ★ ★ ★ ★
22 Rue de Richelieu
1st arrondissement
Phone: 01 42 96 44 50
www.hotel-louvre-piemont.com

This four-star property adjacent lovely Palais Royal, has twenty rooms, recently renovated in an artsy (rather dark) style. Rates run over 300 euros per night, but there are more amenities because it's a four-star hotel.

In their words, "To make your stay even more special, ask for our suite with a balcony! Located on the top floor of the hotel, it offers a unique view of the Palais Royal and has a large bathroom."

HÔTEL LOUVRE SAINTE-ANNE ★ ★ ★
32 Rue Ste. Anne
1st arrondissement
Phone: 01 40 20 02 35
https://paris-hotel-louvre.com/en/

Located east of Avenue de l'Opéra, in a quieter area, near many Japanese fast-food restaurants. Because it's a bit off the beaten track, the prices are better, but it's a small hotel so you need to grab a room quickly if you're interested. The décor features fabrics in warm colors.

The charming breakfast area is in a stone-vaulted cellar. The top floor rooms aren't reachable by elevator.

HÔTEL MONTPENSIER ★ ★
12 Rue de Richelieu
1st arrondissement
Phone: 01 42 96 28 50
www.hotelmontpensierparis.com

In addition to being a sentimental favorite, since this hotel is next door to an apartment I stayed in for three months while writing my first Paris guide, the location can't be beat, especially for the good price, since it's a two-star hotel. If you're looking for value for money, this is it. The two-star rating means it's not as luxurious as other listings (has more of a "budget" feel), but it makes up for that luxury with its warm welcome.

HÔTEL THÉRÈSE ★ ★ ★
5/7 Rue Thérèse
1st arrondissement
Phone: 01 42 96 10 01
www.hoteltherese.com

A stone's throw from Palais Royal, this three-star hotel feels like four-star luxury. The reception staff offers a warm welcome: there is complimentary flavored water in the lobby and the sitting area is plush and intimate, like being in someone's home. The rooms are small, but beautifully decorated, spotlessly clean, and the bath is top notch (marble, nice guest soaps and lotions, plush towels). Very good value for the price.

A nearby restaurant I recommend is Bistrot Vivienne, two blocks away on Rue des Petits Champs.

TIMHOTEL PALAIS ROYAL ★ ★ ★

3 Rue de la Banque
2nd arrondissement
Phone: 01 42 61 53 90
www.timhotel.com

This hotel qualifies as a bargain for the reasonably-priced rooms in a good location, with 24-hour receptionist and attentive staff. The forty-six rooms are small but cute and clean (and importantly, most are reached by an elevator, after a few steps).

A hearty breakfast runs about 15 euros and includes pastries, hot drinks, juice, eggs, cereal, yogurt, fruit, cheese, and ham.

Tuileries Métro Sign

Map #1—First Arrondissement

Palais Royal/Louvre
& St. Honoré/Tuileries

These hotels are in the first arrondissement. The numbers correspond with the numbers on the facing map. Their listings and descriptions are found in chapters one and two.

1. Hôtel de la Place du Louvre
2. Hôtel Louvre Piemont
3. Hôtel Louvre Sainte-Anne
4. Hôtel Montpensier
5. Hôtel Thérèse
6. Timhotel Palais Royal
7. Hôtel Lion d'Or
8. Hôtel Londre Saint-Honoré
9. Hôtel Relais Saint-Honoré
10. Hôtel Royal Saint-Honoré
11. Hôtel Saint-Roch

Tuileries Gardens

CHAPTER TWO

ST. HONORÉ/TUILERIES

This area is also near the Louvre Museum, a bit closer to Place de la Concorde. You'll find the Place du Marché Saint-Honoré with lots of trendy restaurants, designer stores on Rue St. Honoré, and arcade shops on Rue de Rivoli. The Tuileries Gardens stretch from the Louvre to Musée de l'Orangerie (which showcases Claude Monet's wall-size water lily paintings).

A major Métro Line #1 takes you to the Champs-Élysées and Arc de Triomphe in one direction and Notre-Dame in the other.

Hôtel Lion d'Or
Hôtel Londre Saint-Honoré
Hôtel Relais Saint-Honoré
Hôtel Royal Saint-Honoré
Hôtel Saint-Roch

HÔTEL LION D'OR ★ ★ ★
5 Rue de la Sourdiere
1st arrondissement
Phone: 01 42 60 79 04
https://www.hotelduliondor.com/en/

In a great location on a quiet side street, this hotel is a bargain price for the high-rent district. Place du Marché Saint-Honoré is nearby, as are wine bars and great shops. Rue St. Honoré is at the end of the block. They are known for charming service and attention to detail. Rooms have been renovated in the past few years.

HÔTEL LONDRE SAINT-HONORÉ ★ ★ ★
13 Rue St. Roch
1st arrondissement
Phone: 01 42 60 15 62
http://www.hotellondressthonore-paris.com/en/

I have been recommending this decently-priced hotel for the neighborhood for decades and am glad to see it's still offering visitors good value for a great location, opposite Église Saint-Roch (where the bells chime regularly, very atmospheric). The twenty-eight rooms have been refurbished, although it's not the height of luxury—more a comfortable place to stay without breaking the bank. Even though it's a three-star, there is a steep staircase to reach the elevator.

Their website shares interesting history about this ancient building (including when it crossed paths with King Louis XIV and Napoleon).

HÔTEL RELAIS SAINT-HONORÉ ★ ★ ★ ★
308 Rue St. Honoré
1st arrondissement
Phone: 01 42 96 06 06
https://www.hotel-relais-saint-honore.com/

All the rooms in this charming boutique hotel are beautifully decorated in vibrant colors, elegant drapes, lush linens, attractive throw pillows, a desk, recessed lighting, and attractive art on walls. For a four-star hotel, the prices are reasonable, as low as 325 euros per night on certain dates. And the location can't be beat, seriously. It's a lovely area—designer shops, many restaurants within a few blocks, Tuileries Gardens a block away. Very centrally located.

HÔTEL ROYAL SAINT-HONORÉ ★ ★ ★ ★
221 Rue St. Honoré
1st arrondissement
Phone: 01 42 60 32 79
https://www.hotel-royal-st-honore.com/

This four-star hotel is more luxurious, and more pricey, but they do have some deals on their website (especially if you book a nonrefundable room, which they call "deposit" so read the terms carefully).

Befitting the level of luxury, there is a restaurant and bar in the hotel, which is very convenient. I'll warn you that it's in a shopping mecca, so the nearby designer stores could break your budget. But, hey, it's Paris. And the window shopping is not-to-be-missed.

HÔTEL SAINT-ROCH ★★
25 Rue St. Roch
1st arrondissement
Phone: 01 42 60 17 91
http://www.hotelsaintroch-paris.com/

This hotel fits the "affordable" label. It's small and the rooms are basic, some might even say spartan, but they're clean and non-fussy. Most importantly, the bathrooms have been renovated. If you're set on staying in this area and looking for a bargain, this hotel has some of the lowest rates (around 240 euros per night for a couple during off season). They offer the best rates for non-refundable rooms of three nights' duration or more.

There is an elevator, but you have to climb a flight of stairs to reach reception and the elevator.

CHAPTER THREE

OPÉRA GARNIER

The streets around the breathtaking Opéra Garnier are a busy transportation hub: Gare Saint-Lazare train station nearby, many bus lines on Avenue de l'Opéra, and the Roissy Bus to Charles de Gaulle airport (bus stop next to the Opéra).

Galeries Lafayette department store complex is behind the Opéra. The area has a lot of foot traffic, but if you walk a block or two away from Avenue de l'Opéra you'll find lovely squares with cafés and smaller neighborhood shops.

    Hôtel Ascot Opéra
    Hôtel Choiseul Opéra
    Hôtel Edouard 7
    Hôtel Île-de-France Opéra
    Hôtel Louvre Marsollier Opéra

Opéra Garnier Façade

HÔTEL ASCOT OPÉRA ★ ★ ★
2 Rue Monsigny
2nd arrondissement
Phone: 01 42 96 87 66
https://www.ascotparishotel.com/

A three-star hotel with the décor of a four-star hotel, they offer very good rates, around 240 euros per night off season for the entry-level double. Rooms aren't big, but the artistic décor is lovely and the bathrooms are updated. They also have a bar, convenient for gathering with friends before going out, and they allow pets. Very good location on a side street near Avenue de l'Opéra.

HÔTEL CHOISEUL OPÉRA ★ ★ ★
1 Rue Daunou
2nd arrondissement
Phone: 01 42 61 70 41
https://www.hotelchoiseuloperaparis.com/

Simple, clean lines and furnishings—I find the décor a bit cool, but others may like the modern feel. I'm including this hotel for the good location near Opéra Garnier, only a few blocks from ritzy Place Vendôme. For this upscale area, the prices are reasonable.

HÔTEL EDOUARD 7 ★ ★ ★ ★
39 Avenue de l'Opéra
2nd arrondissement
Phone: 01 42 61 56 90
https://www.hoteledouard7-paris.com/

For a four-star splurge in the Opéra area, Hôtel Edouard 7 offers a central location on the Avenue, a fancy restaurant, and some rooms with balconies. Deals can be found for around 400 euros per night on certain dates, a very good price for the luxurious surroundings, upscale amenities and service. It is a noisy area, so if that is a concern for you, request a quiet room.

HÔTEL ÎLE-DE-FRANCE OPÉRA ★ ★ ★
26 Rue Saint-Augustin
2nd arrondissement
Phone: 01 47 42 40 61
https://www.iledefrance-paris-hotel.com/

Beautiful décor, attentive service, and very good prices; some of the best I've seen for the area. Love the location above Avenue de l'Opéra in a quiet area, but still near everything.

In their words, "Hôtel Île-de-France Opéra is located in an elegant eighteenth-century townhouse with an interesting history: Louise de La Vallière, who became mistress to Louis XIV, the Sun King, lived here when in Paris. She was seventeen and a maid-of-honor to Louis' brother's wife when the king wooed her."

HÔTEL LOUVRE MARSOLLIER OPÉRA ★ ★ ★
13 Rue Marsollier
2nd arrondissement
Phone: 01 42 96 68 14
www.hotellouvremarsollier.com

Currently under renovation, rooms are on the small side but the location is excellent and the prices are very reasonable for the area.

Just north of Avenue de l'Opéra, near Place Gaillon, this hotel gem is in a somewhat quieter area. Place Gaillon nearby boasts a mouth-watering patisserie and a couple of gourmet restaurants.

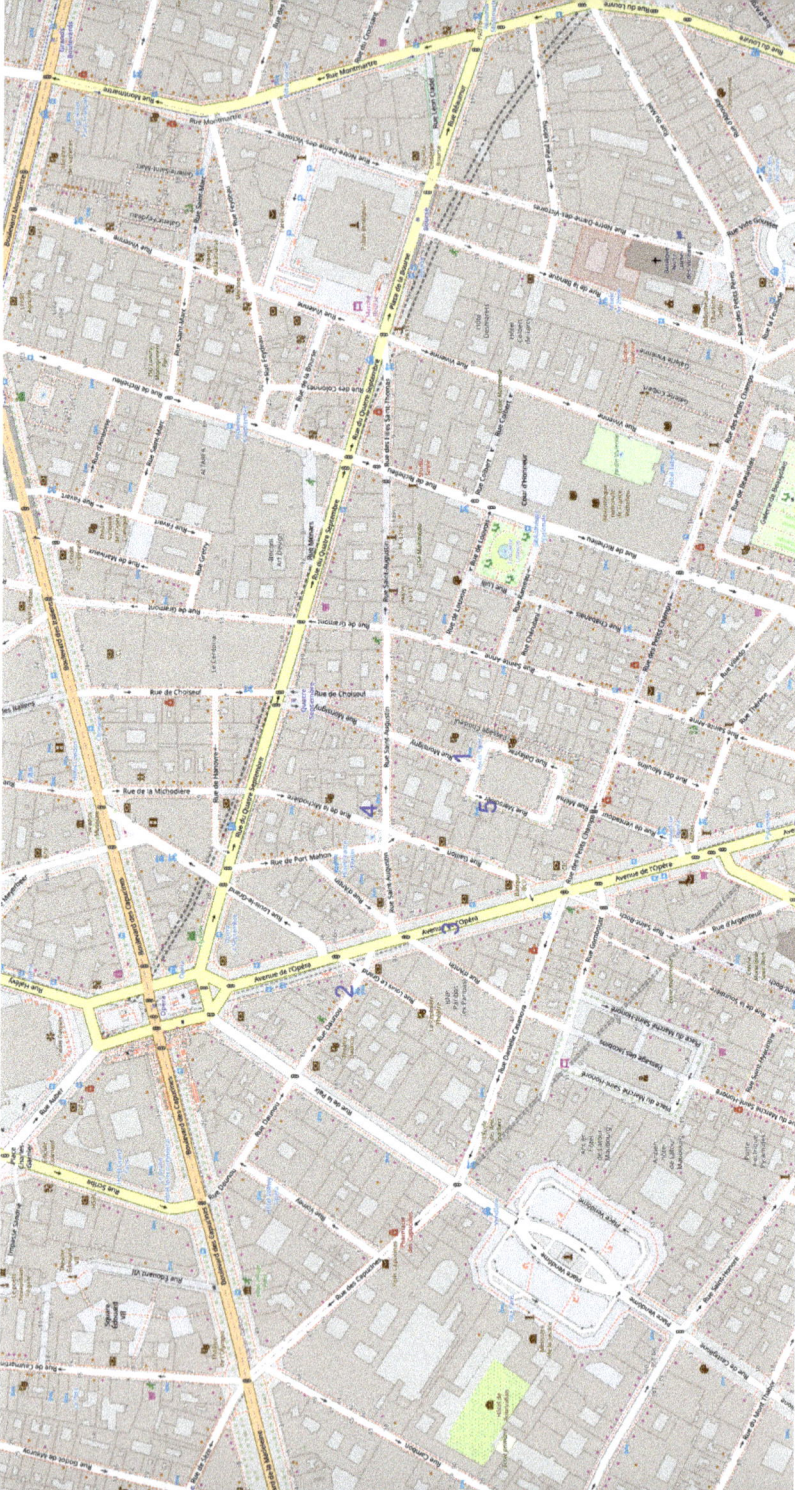

Map #2—Second Arrondissement

Opéra Garnier

These hotels are in the second arrondissement. The numbers correspond with the numbers on the facing map. Their listings and descriptions are found in chapter three.

1. Hôtel Ascot Opéra
2. Hôtel Choiseul Opéra
3. Hôtel Edouard 7
4. Hôtel Île de France Opéra
5. Hôtel Louvre Marsollier Opéra

Sainte-Chappelle on Île de la Cité

CHAPTER FOUR

MARAIS /
ÎLE SAINT-LOUIS

The historic Marais district is rich in history and includes Paris's oldest square—Place des Vosges, built in 1604 by King Henry IV. There are two world-class museums: Musée Carnavalet, depicting the long history of Paris, and Musée Picasso.

In the same arrondissement, you'll find Île Saint-Louis, a small island that exudes romantic ambience. The main street is lined with interesting boutiques, intimate cafés, and the famous Berthillon ice cream shop. The impressive Notre-Dame Cathedral towers a short distance away on adjoining Île de la Cité. Generally, Paris hotel rooms are small, but on Île Saint-Louis, the rooms are *très petite* because space is at a premium.

Hôtel Caron de Beaumarchais
Hôtel Caron Le Marais
Hôtel de Neuve
Hôtel du Jeu de Paume
Hôtel des Deux-Îles
Hôtel Jeanne d'Arc
Hôtel Saint-Louis en l'Isle

HÔTEL CARON DE BEAUMARCHAIS ★★★
12 Rue Vielle du Temple
4th arrondissement
Phone: 01 42 72 34 12
https://www.carondebeaumarchais.com/en/

Small boutique hotel on a quiet street near Place Sainte-Catherine. Bit off the beaten tourist track. The rooms are small but beautifully appointed in muted colors; some have balconies. The refurbished bathrooms are modern and designy. Atmospheric breakfast room with stone walls. Prices are very good, around 225 euros per night, if you book ahead. They're billing themselves as "a budget hotel," so they're cognizant of Paris price shock.

In their words, "…museum hotel with a piano-forte of 1792, a harp—reminding that Beaumarchais was the harp teacher of Louis XV's daughters…" Note: If you have mobility issues, there are three steps to reach the elevator, and the first few steps don't have a railing.

HÔTEL CARON LE MARAIS ★ ★ ★
3 Rue Caron
4th arrondissement
Phone: 01 40 29 02 95
https://www.hotelcaron.com/

This boutique hotel, only eighteen rooms, has modern décor and colorful accents. Rooms are on the small side, but they do include a minibar with free snacks.

The atmospheric stone-vaulted breakfast room offers a buffet of pastries, cereal, juice, eggs, etc. Nearby, there are several restaurants with outdoor patios.

HÔTEL DE NEUVE ★ ★ ★
14 Rue Neuve Saint-Pierre
4th arrondissement
Phone: 01 44 59 28 50
https://www.hoteldeneuveparis.com/

Pretty rooms in what they call "chic and contemporary baroque style." Nice bathrooms with heated towel racks; some have tubs. Attractive lobby, with plush seating and bookshelves, and an outdoor terrace with tables and chairs.

Reasonable rates and best prices on their website.

Excellent location near Place des Vosges. Great ratings from travelers.

HÔTEL DU JEU DE PAUME ★ ★ ★ ★
54 Rue St. Louis en l'Île
4th arrondissement
Phone: 01 43 26 14 18
https://www.jeudepaumehotel.com/en/

This four-star hotel is normally pricier than the three-star listings, but there are deals to be had (around 300 euros per night off season). If you can find one of those, I'd grab it. It's a luxurious hotel in a perfect location. The elegantly appointed rooms are on the small side, but very artistic.

There are also lovely public seating areas; feels as if you're being invited into someone's home. The entrance is via an outdoor courtyard.

HÔTEL DES DEUX-ÎLES ★ ★ ★
59 Rue St. Louis en l'Île
4th arrondissement
Phone: 01 43 26 13 35
https://www.deuxiles-paris-hotel.com/

Hôtel des Deux-Îles has undergone quite a transformation since I reported on it for my first Paris guide. Then it was a basic hotel in a great location. Now, it is a gorgeous hotel with yummy décor—nice fabrics, floral spray motifs, and lovely watercolors.

The cozy salon with an "honesty wine bar" is lined with bookshelves. Guests can enjoy complimentary "tea time" in the afternoon. Reasonable prices for the location.

HÔTEL JEANNE D'ARC ★★★

3 Rue de Jarente
4th arrondissement
Phone: 01 48 87 62 11
https://hoteljeannedarc.com/

Located in a quiet area near Place des Vosges, there are many shops and restaurants in the neighborhood. The décor is basic, not luxurious. Neat and clean. Good prices for the area and "best rate guarantee" on their website. No air conditioning, just fans in the rooms.

Recommended by regular travelers to Paris.

HÔTEL SAINT-LOUIS EN L'ISLE ★★★

75 Rue St. Louis en l'Île
4th arrondissement
Phone: 01 46 34 04 80
https://www.saintlouisenlisle.com/en/

This beautiful hotel is fully renovated in subdued shades, boasts marble baths, and features nice linens. There are large windows (many with good views), and some rooms have balconies with a table and chairs. All rooms have a minibar and courtesy tray with hot drinks and cookies.

Lovely breakfast room with stone walls and vaulted ceiling. After breakfast, the hotel offers complimentary tea and coffee in lounge. They have many repeat customers.

Map #3—Fourth Arrondissement

Marais / Île Saint-Louis

These hotels are in the fourth arrondissement. The numbers correspond with the numbers on the facing map. Their listings and descriptions are found in chapter four.

1. Hôtel Caron Le Marais
2. Hôtel de Neuve
3. Hôtel du Jeu de Paume
4. Hôtel des Deux-Îles
5. Hôtel Jeanne d'Arc
6. Hôtel Saint-Louis en l'Île
7. Le Caron de Beaumarchais

Notre-Dame Cathedral

CHAPTER FIVE

LATIN QUARTER

Home to the Sorbonne University, which dates back to the Middle Ages, the area has a student, bohemian vibe that is popular with visitors. Hotel prices are more reasonable, reflecting the relaxed atmosphere. It is also fairly central to sites, especially Notre-Dame.

The lovely Musée de Cluny is in the midst of the action with a charming small park next to it. I've listed hotels on the smaller streets, off Blvd. St. Michel. I don't recommend hotels on that boulevard, which is very noisy and busy and somewhat rundown.

Hôtel Central Saint-Germain
Hôtel Claude Bernard Saint-Germain
Hôtel du College de France
Hôtel du Levant
Hôtel Europe Saint-Severin

HÔTEL CENTRAL SAINT-GERMAIN ★★★
3 Rue Champollion
5th arrondissement
Phone: 01 46 34 14 20
https://www.hotelcentralsaintgermain.fr/en/

Located in a lively area, request a quiet room if that's important to you. The upside is there are many restaurants nearby. The thirty-five renovated rooms are basic, in subdued colors, no frills. Nice breakfast buffet. You can find some deals with good prices.

HÔTEL CLAUDE BERNARD ST-GERMAIN ★★★
43 Rue des Écoles
5th arrondissement
Phone: 01 43 26 32 52
https://www.hotelclaudebernardparis.com/en/

I like the immediate area. There is a bike rental rack in front of the hotel. Directly across the street, you'll find a small gourmet chocolate shop (where you can see the chocolatier at work in the back). A college next to the hotel has a garden with mature trees.

The rooms' simple décor is a bit heavy on velvet for my taste. The breakfast room is basic with plastic chairs. Best rate on website.

HÔTEL DU COLLÈGE DE FRANCE ★ ★ ★

7 Rue Thénard
5th arrondissement
Phone: 06 58 53 76 04
https://www.hotel-collegedefrance.com/en/

The rooms are a bit dated, basic décor, not luxurious. But the hotel is noted for its friendliness and gets good ratings on all the booking sites, so they're focused on customer service.

Some rooms have balconies, and you need to take stairs to reach the top sixth floor (rest are reached by an elevator).

HÔTEL DU LEVANT ★ ★ ★

18 Rue de la Harpe
5th arrondissement
Phone: 01 46 34 11 00
https://hoteldulevant.com/

This is my top recommendation for the area. The hotel is in a great location near the Seine River, and a popular pedestrian area is nearby with shops, crêperies, etc.

The rooms in this "hôtel de charme" are lovely—luxurious fabrics and colors, matching throw pillows, a desk in each room. They get many repeat guests, and the prices are reasonable.

HÔTEL EUROPE SAINT-SEVERIN ★ ★ ★
38-40 Rue St Severin
5th arrondissement
Phone: 01 46 34 05 70
https://hoteleurope.net/en/

The big plus for this hotel is the great location next to the river. It is also near the pedestrian area, and an Italian restaurant is on the ground floor. Prices are a bit higher than the other listings.

The rooms run on the small side and have simple, warm décor. Some rooms have balconies with views. They do have the option of "bed and half board" reservations that include dinner in the Italian restaurant.

Boat on Seine River

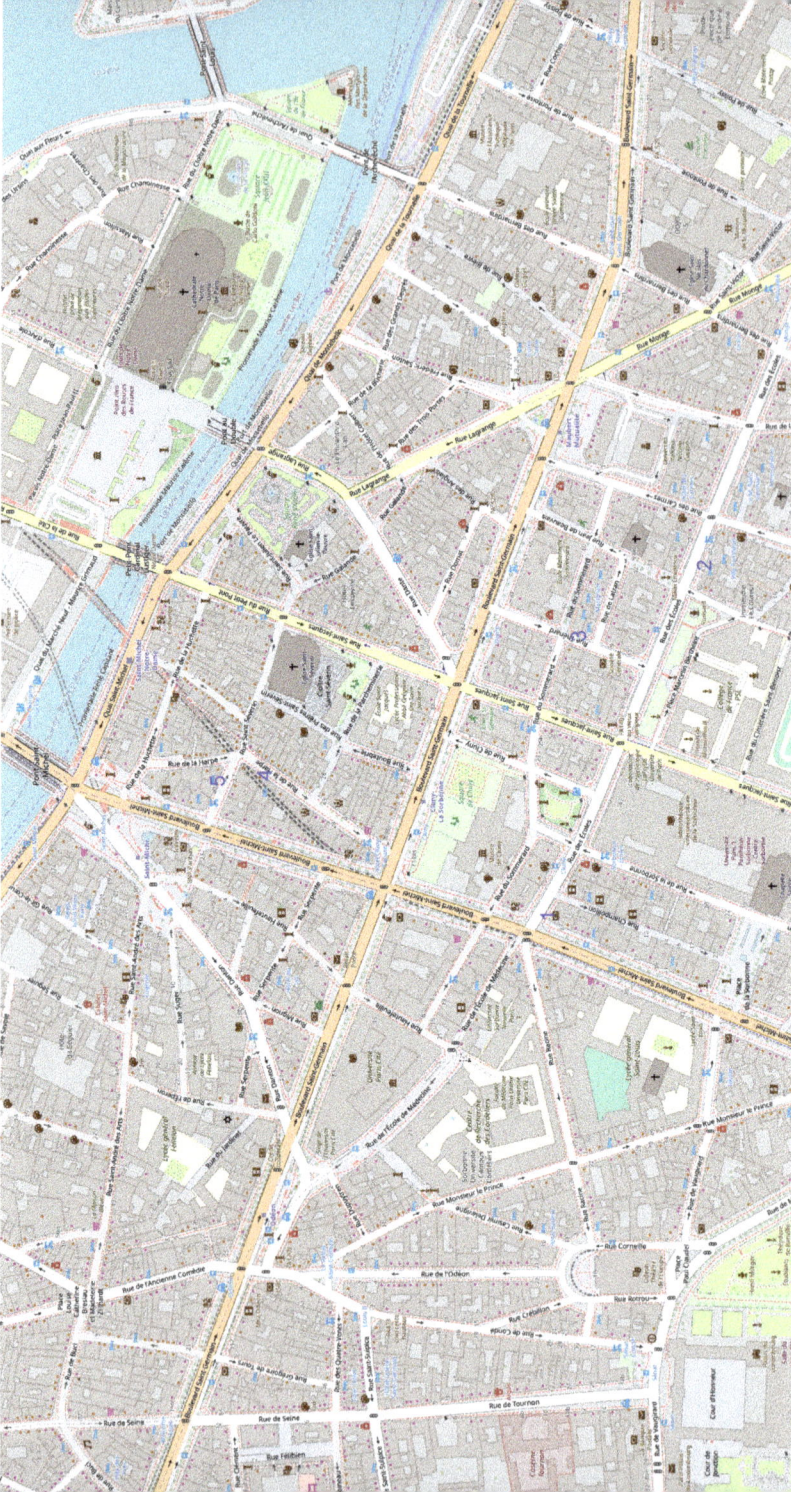

Map #4—Fifth Arrondissement

Latin Quarter

These hotels are in the fifth arrondissement. The numbers correspond with the numbers on the facing map. Their listings and descriptions are found in chapter five.

1. Hôtel Central Saint-Germain
2. Hôtel Claude Bernard Saint-Germain
3. Hôtel du College de France
4. Hôtel du Levant
5. Hôtel Europe Saint-Severin

Église Saint-Germain

CHAPTER SIX

LEFT BANK NEAR SEINE RIVER

The next three chapters are on the Left Bank in Saint-Germain-des-Prés.

This area, on the border closest to the Seine, is convenient to walk to the bridge going over to the Louvre, and in the other direction, the bridge to the larger island and Notre-Dame Cathedral. There are not as many restaurants and boutiques in the immediate vicinity, except for the very busy *Quai* (street) along the Seine.

> Citadines Saint-Germain
> Hôtel Dauphine Saint-Germain
> Hôtel Prince de Conti

CITADINES SAINT-GERMAIN ★ ★ ★ ★
53 Ter., Quai des Grands Augustins
6th arrondissement
Phone: 01 44 07 70 00
https://www.discoverasr.com/en/citadines/france/

This "apart hotel" has studios and one-bedroom apartments. All have kitchenettes, and there is a small fitness center. There is a 24-hour reception desk, like a normal hotel, and continental breakfast in the breakfast room, but the rooms are bigger than a normal hotel.

Clean, simple lines, modern décor. Bit austere for me. A big benefit is the location and kitchenette. Good for families that want a small apartment with a separate bedroom. It doesn't have four-star luxury.

HÔTEL DAUPHINE SAINT-GERMAIN ★ ★ ★
36 Rue Dauphine
6th arrondissement
Phone: 01 43 26 74 34
https://dauphine-st-germain.com/

Pretty rooms, charming locale, feels like a four-star hotel, but with better prices. In their words, this seventeenth-century building "has been carefully refurbished to preserve all the charm and refinement of that beautiful period whilst ensuring modern comfort…" The thirty rooms and suites have exposed beams, luxurious fabrics, and high-quality bedding.

One of my favorite tearooms, Mariages Frères, is a block away (take Rue Christine).

Mariages Frères Tearoom

HÔTEL PRINCE DE CONTI ★ ★ ★

8 Rue Guenegaud
6th arrondissement
Phone: 01 44 07 30 40
https://princedeconti.com/en/

The public spaces are lovely, including a bar area with a fireplace ("courtesy bar" to serve yourself) and a separate charming breakfast room.

The hotel is undergoing renovations as this guide is going to print. We can assume the twenty-four rooms will be updated and the prices may go up.

It is near the river, next to the Monnaie complex which houses a wonderful museum on the French Mint (makes coins) and gourmet restaurant Guy Savoy.

La Palette Café

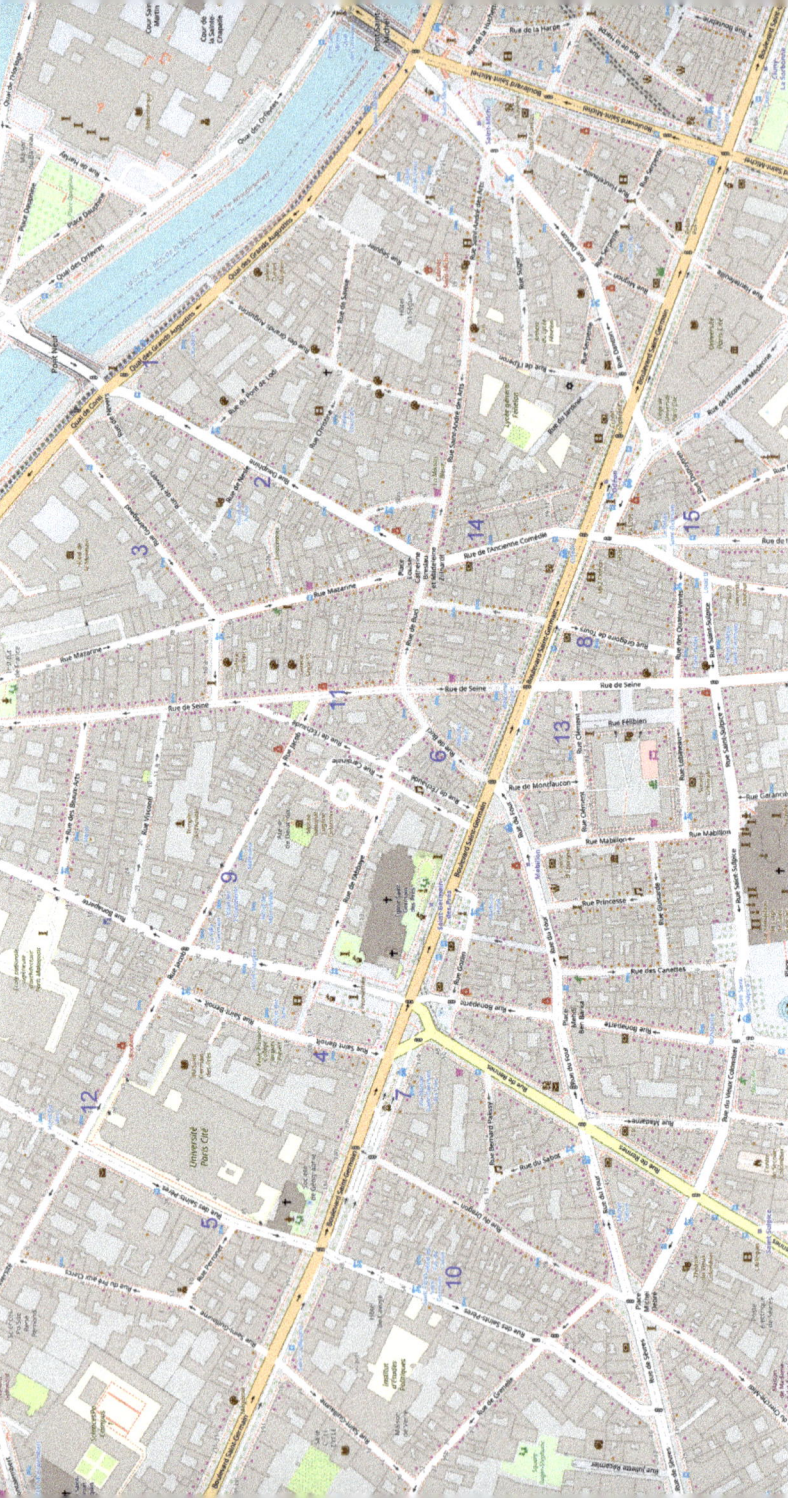

Map #5—Sixth Arrondissement

Saint-Germain-des-Prés

These hotels are in the sixth arrondissement. The numbers correspond with the numbers on the facing map. Their listings and descriptions are found in chapters six and seven.

1. Citadines Saint-Germain
2. Hôtel Dauphine Saint-Germain
3. Hôtel Prince de Conti
4. Crystal Hôtel
5. Hôtel Académie Saint-Germain
6. Hôtel Artus
7. Hôtel au Manoir Saint-Germain
8. Hôtel de Fleurie
9. Hôtel des Marronniers
10. Hôtel des Saints-Pères
11. Hôtel de Seine
12. Hôtel du Danube
13. Hôtel le Clément
14. Hôtel Left Bank Saint-Germain
15. Odéon Hôtel by Malone

CHAPTER SEVEN

LEFT BANK NEAR BLVD. ST. GERMAIN

This is the heart of Saint-Germain-des-Prés and my favorite area in Paris. There are oodles of hotels, because it is *très populaire*. For the past century, the area has been renowned for the writers and artists who frequented local cafés, discussing art, religion, and politics late into the night. Visitors are reminded of that legacy while sipping an espresso at Deux Magots or Café de Flore, browsing art galleries and antique shops, viewing the latest fashions in trendy boutiques, and bargaining with aspiring artists selling their sketches on Blvd St. Germain.

Hotels in the sixth arrondissement reflect this creative, artistic ambience. In high season, foot traffic on the sidewalks becomes crowded. If your schedule allows, it's better to visit in early spring or late fall; prices are better then, as well.

Crystal Hôtel	Hôtel des Marronniers
Hôtel Académie Saint-Germain	Hôtel des Saints-Pères
	Hôtel de Seine
Hôtel Artus	Hôtel du Danube
Hôtel Au Manoir Saint-Germain	Hôtel le Clément
	Hôtel Left Bank Saint-Germain
Hôtel de Fleurie	Odéon Hôtel by Malone

CRYSTAL HÔTEL ★★★
24 Rue St. Benoît
6th arrondissement
Phone: 01 45 48 85 14
https://hotelcrystalsaintgermainparis.com/

Located on a charming street, half a block from Blvd. St. Germain, the area can't be beat. Café de Flore is at the end of the block, and Alain Ducasse Chocolatier is next door.

Excellent prices for the swanky neighborhood. Rooms are small and simply decorated. Nice lounge and breakfast room.

HÔTEL ACADÉMIE SAINT-GERMAIN ★★★★
32 Rue des Saints-Pères
7th arrondissement (on border with 6th arrondissement)
Phone: 01 45 49 80 00
https://academiehotel.com/en/

Befitting its four-star status, this is an elegant, beautiful hotel in a great location adjacent Blvd. St. Germain, near all the Left Bank shops and dining.

I'm a big fan of the classy décor, nice art, period furniture, and hardwood floors. Definitely worth a splurge, and the smaller Standard Room has good prices.

HÔTEL ARTUS ★ ★ ★ ★

34 Rue de Buci
6th arrondissement
Phone: 01 43 29 07 20
https://en.artushotel.com/

Located on busy Rue de Buci, best to request a quiet room. The self-described, "chic atmosphere with fifties accents," feels modern and luxurious.

The bar lounge serves food throughout the day, and the spa offers massage treatments. Reasonable prices for four-star luxury.

In the evening, If you walk a short distance on Rue de Buci, you'll find a lively street scene with café tables filling sidewalks, street performers, and shops open late.

HÔTEL AU MANOIR SAINT-GERMAIN ★ ★ ★ ★

153 Blvd. St. Germain
6th arrondissement
Phone: 01 42 22 21 65
https://www.hotelaumanoir.com/en/

Lives up to the four-star rating with beautiful décor in warm colors, plush fabrics, and elegant furniture. The website has many photos and includes descriptions and size of the rooms.

Lovely breakfast room with wicker chairs, and there is a courtyard. Blvd. St. Germain is very noisy, so request a quiet room (some have garden views). Reasonable prices for a four-star hotel.

HÔTEL DE FLEURIE ★★★

32 Rue Grégoire de Tours
6th arrondissement
Phone: 01 53 73 70 00
https://www.hoteldefleurieparis.com/en/

This three-star hotel borders on four-star luxury. The public spaces and rooms are beautifully decorated in colorful hues with floral wallpaper. Some rooms have balconies.

There is an "honesty bar" in the lounge. My only quibble is that it's more pricey than other three-star listings, running over 300 euros per night for a Classic Double.

A casual restaurant I recommend nearby is Cepe & Figue—hearty French cuisine at great prices.

HÔTEL DES MARRONNIERS ★★★

21 Rue Jacob
6th arrondissement
Phone: 01 43 25 30 60
https://www.hoteldesmarronniers.com/en/

This fully renovated hotel has undergone a major transformation since it's earlier days. Rooms are beautiful and run on the small side.

My favorite feature is the charming outdoor courtyard, which most hotels don't offer. Prices run a bit high, partly due to the demand for this area in the heart of St. Germain shops and restaurants.

HÔTEL DES SAINTS-PÈRES ★ ★ ★ ★
65 Rue des Saints-Pères
6th arrondissement
Phone: 01 45 44 50 00
https://www.esprit-de-france.com/en/hotels/hotel-des-saints-peres

Below Blvd. St. Germain towards Place Saint-Sulpice, this is worth the splurge for the beautiful rooms with high ceilings, large windows, and elegant decorative touches. In their words, "17th- and 18th-century paintings and engravings adorn the walls, making each space unique."

You can enjoy breakfast in the outdoor courtyard, and the bar lounge offers complimentary tea in the afternoon. Prices are higher reflecting the four-star luxury.

HÔTEL DE SEINE ★ ★ ★
52 Rue de Seine
6th arrondissement
Phone: 01 46 34 22 80
https://www.hoteldeseine.com/

Very fancy for a three-star, and with "fancy" prices higher than many other three-star hotels. Beautiful rooms, lovely common areas, great location.

Romantic décor (lots of red).

Even the smallest Classic Room is beautifully decorated with framed art, fabric wall coverings, and marble bath with tub/shower.

HÔTEL DU DANUBE ★ ★ ★
58 Rue Jacob
6th arrondissement
Phone: 01 42 60 34 70
https://www.hoteldanube.fr/en/

My top choice for the area, for the reasonable prices, great location, and quality of the lovely rooms. Speaking from personal experience, the service is excellent. The Classic Double rooms are small but nicely decorated, and many have large windows opening onto the inner courtyard. All rooms have Nespresso coffeemakers.

A charming breakfast room has a plush seating area, in addition to bistro chairs, or you can dine on the outside patio next to potted palms. They allow pets.

HÔTEL LE CLÉMENT ★ ★
6 Rue Clément
6th arrondissement
Phone: 01 43 26 53 60
https://en.hotel-clement.com/

Great location facing the St. Germain covered market.

The small rooms have lovely décor—basically three-star design for two-star prices. A compact elevator serves all six floors. A few rooms have additional steps.

The breakfast features fresh fruit from the nearby market. There is a public swimming pool across the street.

Caroline's cat at Hôtel du Danube

HÔTEL LEFT BANK SAINT-GERMAIN ★★★
9 Rue de l'Ancienne Comédie
6th arrondissement
Phone: 01 43 54 01 70
https://www.hotelleftbank.com/en/

This hotel exudes old-world charm—attractive wall coverings, colorful cushions, and nice wood accents. Bathrooms feature colored marble. Some rooms have another bed in an alcove. Good prices for the area.

Breakfast is discounted on their website, and it gets good feedback from visitors.

ODÉON HÔTEL BY MALONE ★★★
3 Rue de l'Odéon
6th arrondissement
Phone: 01 43 25 90 67
https://odeonhotel.fr/en/

Beautifully decorated hotel, although the Classic Rooms are a bit basic. The higher categories have fabric-covered walls with matching pillows and throws on the bed. They say best rate and breakfast included if you book on their site.

In their words, "At any time from six p.m. to midnight you can enjoy a moment of conviviality by helping yourself to our selection of aperitifs, digestives, wines, champagnes and non-alcoholic drinks, available in our salon. The principle of our honesty bar is simple: feel free to use it as you would at home, then complete the form and leave it at the reception."

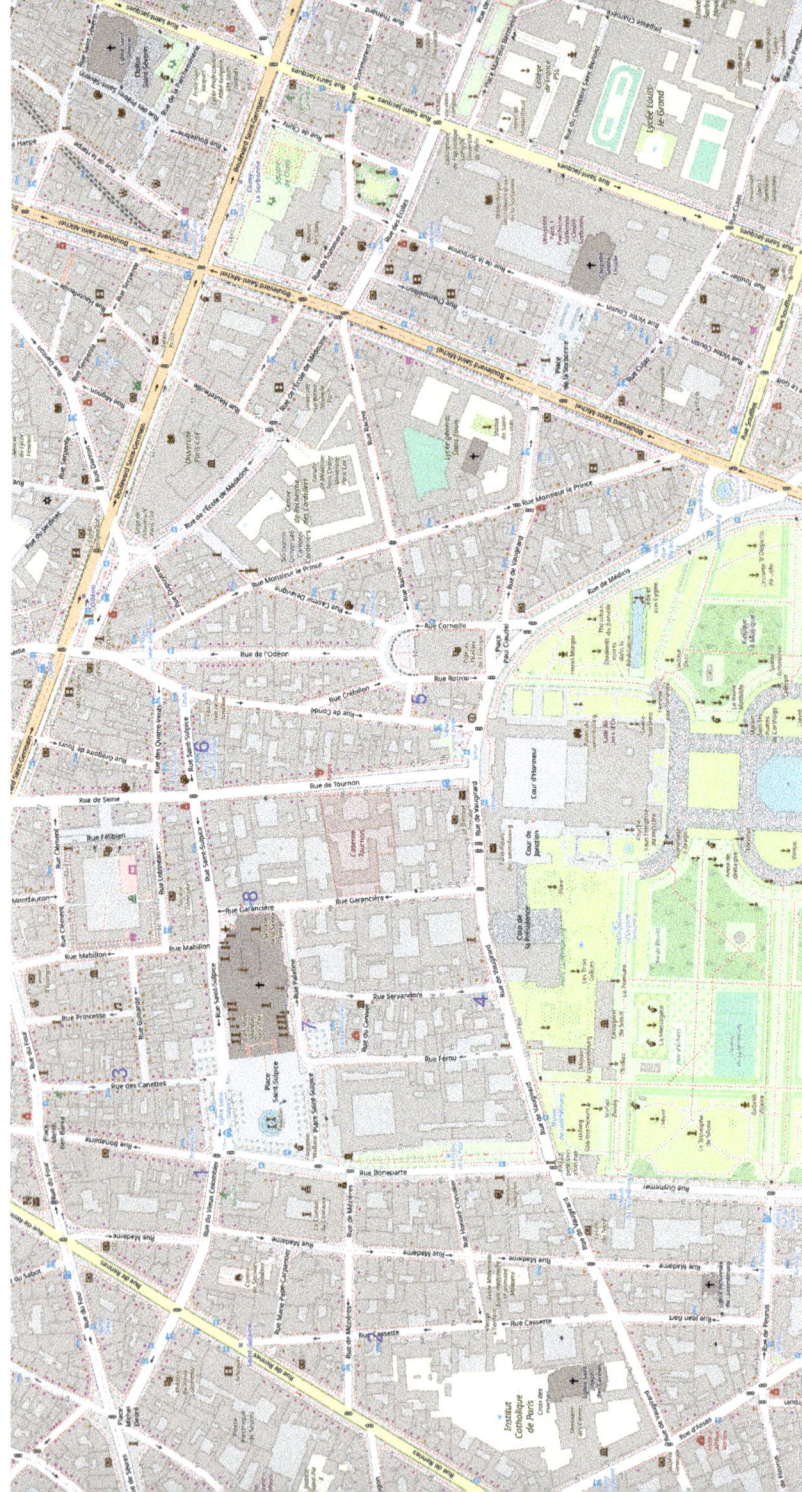

Map #6—Sixth Arrondissement

Place Saint-Sulpice / Luxembourg Gardens

These hotels are in the sixth arrondissement. The numbers correspond with the numbers on the facing map. Their listings and descriptions are found in chapter eight.

1. Hôtel Atlantis
2. Hôtel de l'Abbayé
3. Hôtel La Perle
4. Hôtel Luxembourg Parc
5. Hôtel Michelet Odéon
6. Hôtel Odéon Saint-Germain
7. Hôtel Récamier
8. Hôtel Relais Saint-Sulpice

Église Saint-Sulpice

PLACE SAINT-SULPICE / LUXEMBOURG GARDENS

Place Saint-Sulpice is a hidden gem known by frequent travelers to Paris. The beautiful square in front of Église Saint-Sulpice boasts a fountain surrounded by chestnut trees and benches. High-end shops encircle the square.

Nearby, the Luxembourg Gardens, a large 56-acre park, are perfect for strolling, a morning run, or curling up with a book. The Musée du Luxembourg, an intimate space, hosts world-class exhibits. A branch of renowned Angelina Salon de Thé is next door, serving a light lunch or mid-afternoon gourmet dessert and tea.

> Hôtel Atlantis
> Hôtel de l'Abbayé
> Hôtel La Perle
> Hôtel Luxembourg Parc
> Hôtel Michelet Odéon
> Hôtel Odéon Saint-Germain
> Hôtel Récamier
> Hôtel Relais Saint-Sulpice

HÔTEL ATLANTIS★★★

4 Rue du Vieux Columbier
6th arrondissement
Phone: 01 45 48 31 81
https://www.hotelatlantisparis.com/en/

I'm including this hotel for the great location on a charming block next to Place Saint-Sulpice. The hotel is more like a two-star in terms of décor and comfort. So, I would only book here IF you find a good deal on the price. Otherwise, I'd pick a more luxurious hotel in the area.

HÔTEL DE L'ABBAYÉ ★★★★

10 Rue Cassette
6th arrondissement
Phone: 01 45 44 38 11
https://www.hotelabbayeparis.com/

A Left Bank favorite among visitors to Paris for the beautiful accommodations and warm welcome. Prices are higher, commensurate with the four-star rating, but worth the splurge. The lobby lounge and outdoor garden are gorgeously designed.

In their words, "The Hôtel de l'Abbayé is built on a former Benedictine convent. The 43 rooms and suites of this mansion overlook a private garden, housing a tearoom where you can eat throughout the day."

HÔTEL LA PERLE ★ ★ ★

14 Rue des Canettes
6th arrondissement
Phone: 01 43 29 10 10
https://www.hotel-paris-laperle.com/en/

Another popular hotel in the area. The lovely rooms are four-star quality—beautiful fabrics, plush seating, elegant touches, and beamed ceilings. Very nice bathrooms.

Guests enjoy a beautiful garden terrace room for breakfast and lounging. There is also a bar with a fireplace. Very good prices for the quality.

HÔTEL LUXEMBOURG PARC ★ ★ ★ ★

42 Rue de Vaugirard
6th arrondissement
Phone: 01 53 10 36 50
https://www.luxembourg-paris-hotel.com/en/

Befitting the four-star category, the gorgeous rooms feature plushly-upholstered chairs, beautiful drapes, and nicely framed paintings on the walls. Some rooms have terraces outside large double doors. The elegant breakfast room has linen-draped tables.

In their words, "Hôtel Luxembourg Parc combines the timeless allure of Louis XV and Napoleon III styles. Treat yourself to luxury and well-being in our well-equipped fitness room."

HÔTEL MICHELET ODÉON ★ ★ ★
6 Place de l'Odéon
6th arrondissement
Phone: 01 53 10 05 60
https://www.hotelmicheletodeon.com/en/

Located steps from the Luxembourg Gardens, the décor is not as plush as many of the other listings, but it's clean and neat with nice warm colors. And the prices can't be beat. This is value for money in a very good location. A note—bathrooms are renovated but not fancy.

They indicate that best prices are on their website and include breakfast.

HÔTEL ODÉON SAINT-GERMAIN ★ ★ ★ ★
13 Rue Saint-Sulpice
6th arrondissement
Phone: 01 43 25 70 11
https://www.hotelparisodeonsaintgermain.com/en/

Great location! Beautiful rooms. Good prices. In their words, "The hotel was built in 1530. Our world-famous decorator, Jacques Garcia, entirely renovated the hotel in 2024, plunging it back in time, boasting its original white beams and visible cut stone ... A palette of prune, greyish beige, golden ochre and orange."

I'm a big fan of Jacques Garcia, so I love this décor in dark, earthy tones, very luxe. And for a four-star hotel, the rates are good.

HÔTEL RÉCAMIER ★ ★ ★ ★
3 bis Place Saint-Sulpice
6th arrondissement
Phone: 01 43 26 04 89
https://en.hotelrecamier.com/

Beautiful, but pricey (almost 400 euros per night for Classic Double). And those entry-level rooms don't have coffee makers. Granted, all the rooms are gorgeous; the location is fabulous; and the public space is yummy. If breakfast isn't included in your rate, it's an extra 30 euros per person.

Repeat guests rave about the location, service and comfort, so it's almost like a five-star hotel. They do offer complimentary afternoon tea and pastries in their lovely lounge, and there is a courtyard garden.

HÔTEL RELAIS SAINT-SULPICE ★ ★ ★ ★
3 Rue Garancière
6th arrondissement
Phone: 01 46 33 99 00
https://www.relais-saint-sulpice.com/en/

Honestly, I don't know how this hotel warrants a four-star rating. Many of the rooms are closer to two-star quality, although that could improve. I'm including it for the great location, near Église Saint-Sulpice and the possibility of finding good rates.

Depending on the dates, there are rooms under 200 euros per night. In that case, it could be worth it. Also, it's in a busy area, so if noise is an issue request a room facing the courtyard.

1874 Impressionist Exhibit at Musée d'Orsay

CHAPTER NINE

MUSÉE D'ORSAY

The seventh arrondissement is an upscale residential area, which makes it more peaceful and relaxing. You'll find Parisians going about their daily life, frequenting the neighborhood shops that cater to them. Rue du Bac is one of the loveliest streets in Paris to stroll and enjoy lunch at one of the many restaurants and cafés.

The area surrounding Musée d'Orsay is a mecca for art galleries. There is also an RER station next to the museum where you can catch a fast train to Versailles.

Also nearby is Musée Rodin where sculptor Auguste Rodin created his magnificent works. The building is surrounded by a garden that showcases some of his large masterpieces.

Hôtel de l'Université
Hôtel Saint-Germain

HÔTEL DE L'UNIVERSITÉ ★ ★ ★

22 Rue de l'Université
7th arrondissement
Phone: 01 42 61 09 39
https://www.universitehotel.com/

This hotel is close to Musée d'Orsay and the surrounding elegant design stores and chic cafés.

Simply furnished, no frills, it leans modern and not as luxe as others. The bathroom (and standing shower) in the "Individual Room" is tiny.

In their words, "Most of the rooms are accessible by an elevator, but some require you to take the stairs, so do not hesitate to call us if you wish to have a room completely accessible by elevator."

HÔTEL SAINT-GERMAIN ★ ★ ★ ★

88 Rue du Bac
7th arrondissement
Phone: 01 49 54 70 00
https://www.hotel-saint-germain.fr/

I'm including this hotel for the attractive rooms in a great location. The public space is beautiful, and the breakfast room has a lovely outdoor terrace.

It's not quite as luxurious as most of the other four-star properties, and the rates are expensive during high season, over 400 euros per night. In off season, the rates are competitive, under 300 euros.

Café Gourmand at Les Antiquaires

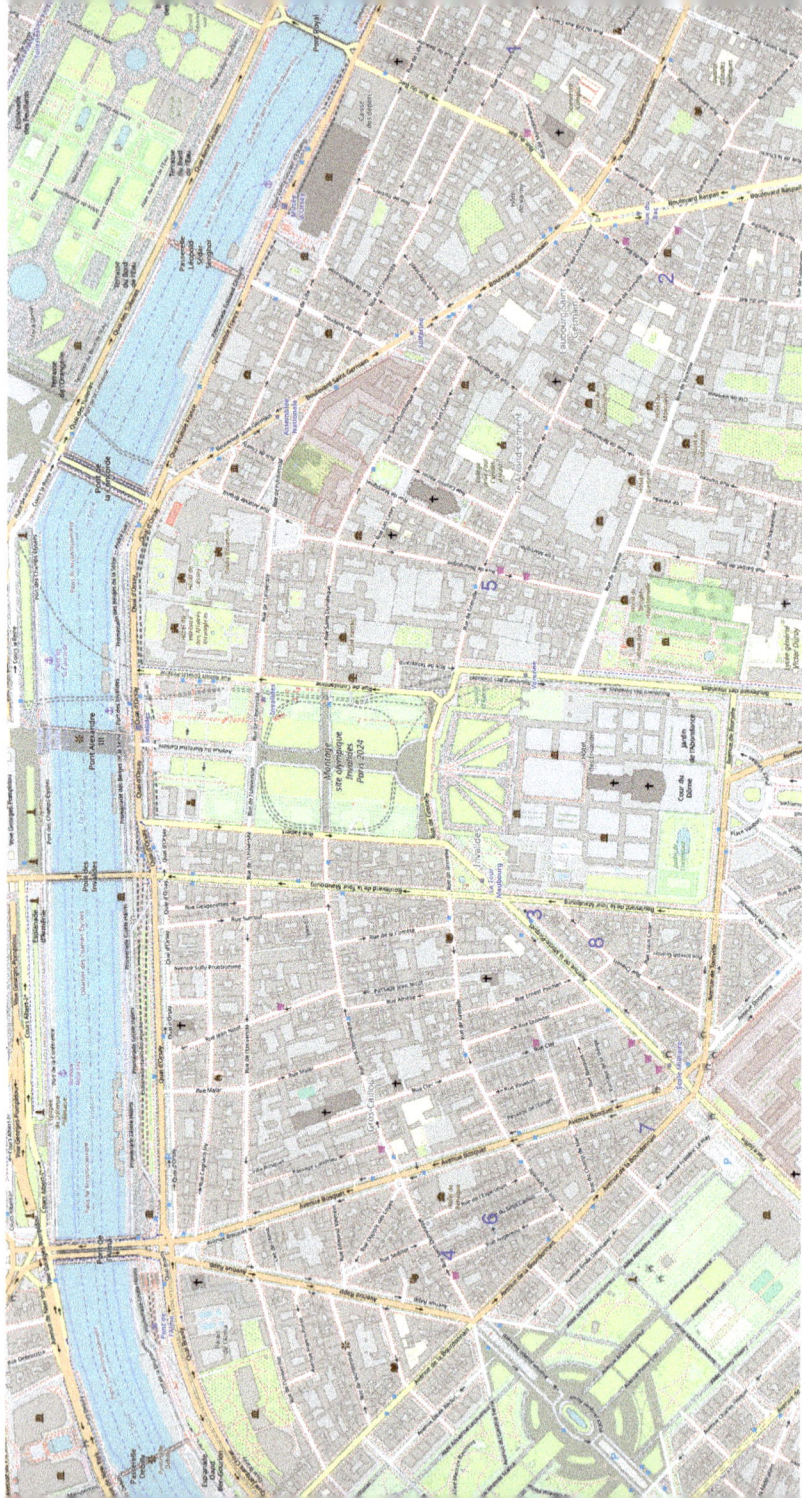

Map #7—Seventh Arrondissement

Musée d'Orsay / Eiffel Tower

These hotels are in the seventh arrondissement. The numbers correspond with the numbers on the facing map. Their listings and descriptions are found in chapters nine and ten.

1. Hôtel de l'Université
2. Hôtel Saint-Germain
3. Hôtel de l'Empereur by Malone
4. Hôtel de Londres Eiffel
5. Hôtel de Varenne
6. Hôtel Eiffel Rive Gauche
7. Hôtel La Bourdonnais
8. Hôtel Muguet

Eiffel Tower

CHAPTER TEN

EIFFEL TOWER

Many visitors say they want to stay near the Eiffel Tower, but I don't think they realize how far it is from other major sites. There are charming cafés and boutiques on Rue St. Dominique, and the Rodin Museum and Hôtel des Invalides are in the area. Prices are a bit higher due to proximity to the Eiffel Tower and the number of four-star hotels in this section.

To get to other parts of Paris, many buses pass by the Eiffel Tower. My favorite is Bus #42 that runs over the Seine River, down elegant Avenue Montaigne to Avenue des Champs-Élysées, then on to Place de la Concorde, and up to Opéra Garnier. This is a scenic bus ride!

Hôtel de l'Empereur By Malone
Hôtel de Londres Eiffel
Hôtel de Varenne
Hôtel Eiffel Rive Gauche
Hôtel La Bourdonnais
Hôtel Muguet

HÔTEL DE L'EMPEREUR BY MALONE ★ ★ ★
2 Rue Chevert
7th arrondissement
Phone: 01 45 55 88 02
https://hotelempereurparis.com/en/

Near Rue Cler and the Eiffel Tower, the area is residential but still close to sites. The lovely rooms have earthtone colors on the walls, with matching floor to ceiling drapes, and attractive wooden furniture. It can be noisy, so request a quiet room.

The reasonable prices run around 250 euros in off season, including breakfast. A complimentary "welcome buffet" is offered each afternoon with pastries and fruit juices.

HÔTEL DE LONDRES EIFFEL ★ ★ ★ ★
1 Rue Augereau
7th arrondissement
Phone: 01 45 51 63 02
https://www.hotel-paris-londres-eiffel.com/en/

Love this hotel in a great location off Rue St. Dominique near the Eiffel Tower in a charming neighborhood. The beautiful rooms have nice decorative touches befitting the four-star luxury.

Repeat visitors rave about the friendly, attentive service, like staying in someone's home. The snazzy website has info on the hotel history, staff, current exhibitions in Paris, and promo codes.

HÔTEL DE VARENNE ★★★★

44 Rue de Bourgogne
7th arrondissement
Phone: 01 45 51 45 55
https://www.hoteldevarenne.com/en/

This nineteenth-century building is close to Musée Rodin. The twenty-six rooms are beautifully decorated in Louis XVI or Empire style, befitting the four-star category—warm colors, luxurious fabrics, and framed botanicals. Some have garden views.

Enjoy a drink at the end of the day in the wood-paneled lounge. There is a small garden where you can have breakfast when weather permits.

HÔTEL EIFFEL RIVE GAUCHE ★★★

6 Rue du Gros Caillou
7th arrondissement
Phone: 01 45 51 51 51
https://hoteleiffelrivegauche.com/en/

The rooms are basic and run on the small side, but the hotel staff is very helpful. I'm including this hotel for the great location off Rue St. Dominique and the good price for the area.

Breakfast is offered for a fee, but I would venture out and find a nearby café. If you're looking for luxury, I'd opt for one of the four-star hotels in this section.

HÔTEL LA BOURDONNAIS ★ ★ ★ ★

Adjacent Champ de Mars
111-113 Avenue de la Bourdonnais
7th arrondissement
Phone: 01 47 05 45 42
https://www.hotellabourdonnais.com/en/

This hotel has a few rooms with views of the Eiffel Tower, which many visitors clamor for. It is beautifully decorated, offers a nice breakfast, and the staff is very friendly. It does have four-star prices, so you're not normally getting a bargain here.

In their words, "La Bourdonnais is named after the famous wig-wearing bird and member of the canary family...Here, exotism, curiosity and exploration reign supreme."

HÔTEL MUGUET ★ ★ ★

11 Rue Chevert
7th arrondissement
Phone: 01 47 05 05 93
https://hotelparismuguet.com/en/

This hotel has bargain prices for the area. It's not as luxurious as many of the three-star hotels in Saint-Germain-des-Prés. Rooms are decorated in grays and reds and run on the small side.

It does get high ratings from guests. For foodies, Rue Cler is nearby; a good option for breakfast.

IN CLOSING

I realize some of these listings may seem pricey. I wanted to include attractive properties that do have deals IF you book ahead, at least six months, and especially if you travel in off season. A rule-of-thumb good price for a charming hotel in a great area is under 250 euros per night. You can't get much better than that in Paris.

Some travel experts say the choice of hotel is not an important element. It's just a place to rest your head at the end of a busy day of sightseeing. I disagree. I think the hotel stay is an integral part of the enjoyment of your trip. It affords you the opportunity to experience the French culture in an intimate way: valuing attentive service from the front desk; appreciating the artistic décor; luxuriating in sumptuous bathrooms with French products; enjoying a gourmet breakfast in charming surroundings; and, most importantly, being in a prime location among Paris's wonderful treasures.

AUTHOR NOTE

My love affair with Paris began on a magical trip with my friend, Leigh, decades ago. We used *Frommer's Guide to Europe on $20 a Day* and found an atmospheric bargain hotel on Rue St. Roch, a block from the Tuileries Gardens, for under $50 per night (with *petit déjeuner* delivered to our door).

That trip inspired many more trips and an extended stay in an apartment on Rue de Richelieu (near the Louvre). As a result, I've written three complete guidebooks to Paris. The latest, *Every Woman's Guide to Romance In Paris*, includes travel advice and information on museums, shops, restaurants and bars, day trips, and a glossary of French terms.

If you're a Francophile like me, you might enjoy my romance novel, *The Champagne Crush* (Sept. 2025), which has scenes in Paris, the Champagne Region, and Bordeaux.

A Request: I would be very grateful for a star rating or short review on Amazon for *Affordable Paris Hotels*.

Free Packing Guide: *Paris Packing Tips* explains how to look glamorous in the City of Light, while traveling light: www.CarolineOC.com.

Lastly, I hope you have a memorable adventure on your next trip to Paris.

Caroline O' Connell

LIST OF PHOTOS
AND MAPS

PHOTOS

Photos ©Caroline O'Connell

MAPS

Map data from ©OpenStreetMap (OSM):
www.OpenStreetMap.org/copyright

INDEX